MW01129509

HOW TO USE A COMPASS FOR KIDS (... AND ADULTS TOO!)

YOUR LITTLE GUIDE TO BECOMING AN EXPERT NAVIGATOR WITH A TRUSTY COMPASS

HENRY D. BRIDGES

Paperback ISBN: 978-3-96772-077-8

Hardcover ISBN: 978-3-96772-078-5

Cover Design by Teofan Gavriliu

The Icons used in this work were from:

- Freepik
- Flaticon

Published by Admore Publishing: Roßbachstraße, Berlin, Germany

Printed in the United States of America

www.admorepublishing.com

CONTENTS

AN INTRODUCTION TO COMPASSES

It's been a long time since most of us used anything other than a GPS to guide us while traveling. On most days, if we look for directions to somewhere new, we pull up a map on a fancy cellphone. So it might seem like the days of paper maps, and compasses are long gone. But the truth is, while your GPS can lose satellite signal and your phone can run out of data, a trusty compass will never let you down.

Compasses work in places that phones and GPS systems don't. They don't need batteries, or line of sight, or a cell-phone signal.

That's because they use the invisible force of **magnetism** that is all around us all the time. Because believe it or not, our planet is kind of like a gigantic magnet itself. So, just like magnets attract and repel each other based on their poles, the earth's polarity affects your compass.

It's science, but it does seem a little like magic!

But unlike magic, it can be explained, and everyone can learn to use it. You don't even need a funny hat and a rabbit. Just your trusty compass and this book will make it easy to master navigation the old school way.

Chances are, most of the people you know don't know how compasses work. It's not exactly a commonly used skill these days. But that doesn't mean it's not worth knowing! In fact, since, as you can see, modern navigation options rely on things like power, cellphone signal, and batteries, a compass lets you go to more places.

While electronics tether you to cities, "old-school" technology like the compass open up the world up for you. A compass can take you to places that you wouldn't be able to find or visit otherwise. It helps you to find your way home from literally anywhere on the planet. That's pretty amazing!

WHAT'S NEXT?

Maybe you've been given a compass. Or maybe you bought one. Maybe you're learning about compasses in school, or you need to use one for a camping trip or something else. Then, you've come to the right place!

In this book, we're going to cover everything you never knew you needed to know about compasses, where they came from, and how they work. We're going to look at simple tips to use your compass correctly and things that might damage it (*so you can avoid that!*) It's part science, part history, and all adventure. Because when you have a compass in your pocket, you can find your way around anywhere!

WHY ME, AND WHY THIS BOOK?

Unlike many people you might know today, I actually grew up before there were GPS units and even before cell phones.

Long before we turned to the internet for everything, I was learning things from books just like this, and I was an avid camper and road tripper. Which means I actually used compasses and maps very often.

I even built my own basic compasses in school science classes, and used them on hiking trips with my troupe as a child, and was the unofficial navigator on long road trips into the unknown.

I'm also a science geek, obsessed with discovering how things work. So, I was always the kid that got in trouble for taking things apart and putting them back together (*not always successfully.*) But, while my mom would argue that she could have done with less of that kind of experimentation,

I've never lost the desire to understand how the world works.

I hope this book inspires you to love science that at first seems a little like magic and to never stop exploring. Literally and figuratively.

WHAT YOU WILL UNCOVER...

Reading this book, you will discover where compasses come from and the science behind how they work. You'll learn what helps compasses work better and what can throw them off. Most importantly, you will discover the correct way to use a compass and how they, along with maps, can help you find nearly anything, anywhere.

This book is a guide, but you still have to do the work, and like anything else, using a compass correctly requires practice. Just knowing the theory is not enough. So, make sure you have a compass that you can practice with while you learn!

ADVENTURE AWAITS

We're nearly ready to get started on the journey of exploring the secrets of the magical compass.

I'm very excited that you're going to learn how to navigate your way around the world with a compass and glad you've chosen this book.

By the time you finish this book, I am sure you will agree with me: that compasses are some of the most exciting and underrated pieces of equipment. Also, knowing how to use one is one of the coolest things you can do.

Once you know how to use a compass, it's a skill you will never lose. Like riding a bicycle! And if you take one with you when you ride your bike, you'll always know exactly where you are – and where you're headed!

So, let's get right into it.

NOT ALL CLASSROOMS
HAVE 4 WALLS...

- Anonymous

CHAPTER 1

WHAT IS A COMPASS?

Compasses work by harnessing science. They use magnetism and the earth's own magnetic field to work. But just being able to say that doesn't mean you know exactly what they are, where they came from, and how they work.

In fact, when it comes to cool scientific tools like a compass, a big part of understanding how they work (and appreciating their genius!) is to understand their history. So, this chapter is part history, part science, and all interesting!

WHAT IS A COMPASS?

A compass (or magnetic compass) is a device that shows direction.

There are simple and complex designs for compasses out there, but in its simplest form, a compass consists of a casing with the directions (north, east, south, and west) marked on it. It also has a magnetic pin that is mounted on a pivot so it can turn easily.

The compass needle always points towards magnetic north, and because we know where magnetic north is, we can figure out where all the other directions are. So, for instance, if you wanted to go west, you would figure out where north is and head towards the left at ninety degrees. As long as north always stays on your right-hand side, you'll be heading west!

This might all still be a bit confusing for now, but not to worry, we will look at everything in a bit more detail later on in the book.

HOW DO COMPASSES WORK?

Compasses work using magnetism.

The needle of your compass is made from magnetized material, which, like every other magnet out there, is attracted or repelled based on the **polarity** of the magnet.

As you already might know, a magnet with like poles will repel each other, while its opposite poles attract each other.

The earth has poles too – in fact, they're even called the "north pole" and the "south pole." Your magnet's needle is the opposite polarity to the north pole, which is why it is always attracted to the earth's magnetic north pole. That's not exactly "true north" (which we will get to in a bit!), but it does always tell you where magnetic north is!

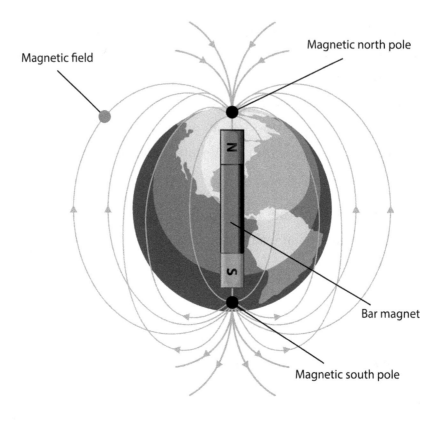

Magnetic field

Magnetic north pole

Bar magnet

Magnetic south pole

So, what you really need to remember when it comes to how compasses work is that the earth is really just one giant magnet – just like the compass in your hand. So, it will always behave the way small magnets do!

Now that we know the essential role magnets play in our compasses, let's learn a bit more about...

THE HISTORY OF MAGNETS AND COMPASSES

Magnets are pretty cool, and we use them in all sorts of things besides compasses. So how did we discover what magnets were, and how we could use them to figure out which way we were going?

We've actually known that magnetism exists for a very long time!

The theory is, that in 77AD, which was 77 years after the year 0, a shepherd in ancient Greece noticed that metal nails were attracted to magnetic rocks. Or at least, the famous naturalist and philosopher known as Pliny the Elder wrote it that way in his book Naturalis Historia!

The ancient Greeks weren't the only ones who recognized and even used magnetism, though. During the Warring States period in China (which happened between 479 and 221 BC), a man named Hanfuzius made the first compass ever. It was known as the *Si Nan*, and instead of pointing north like the modern compasses you and I use, it pointed towards the south!

Next, Chinese sailors also realized that a piece of magnetized steel attached to something that floated like wood or cork, would naturally point towards the north when floated in water.

It took a while for the western world to catch up, but by 1190AD, Alexander Neckham described the same phenomenon. Then by 1269, Pierre de Maricourt had perfected the "dry compass," which worked with the familiar needle mounted on a pin and able to pivot. So something that started to look somewhat similar to the compass you probably have!

Over time, in 1826, we made another HUGE jump with the help of Electromagnets. This is when William Sturgeon first managed to use electricity to create magnetism.

So, when you next look at a compass, remember that we've been using magnets to navigate (*and for many other things!*) for about 2,500 years! That's pretty impressive!

MAPS AND COMPASSES

We can't finish a chapter on how compasses work and where they came from without mentioning their long-time partner: **the map.**

Compasses and maps are like bacon and eggs, or pen and paper. They can exist without each other. But they're much better together!

You've probably seen old maps where there was a drawn compass in one corner (often next to the sea monster that warned old seafarers to avoid dangerous areas!). You still see them on some maps and on things like construction drawings, where you might need to orient yourself north on a building site.

Modern maps, however, are all drawn with north at the top of the map. So, if you are looking at a map the right way up, north is always at the top of the map.

However, just knowing that the top of the map shows what is north of you doesn't help if you don't know which way YOU are heading. Which is why you need a compass.

When you want to use a map and compass together, the best way to do it is to first find north, point yourself in that direction, and then lay your map flat, with the compass on top of it. Adjust as necessary until the top of the map matches the direction your compass says is north. Then you know you're reading the map correctly.

Now, I'm pretty sure you won't always WANT to go north, but once you know where north is, you can easily find out where south, east, and west are, and you can orient yourself accordingly. If you're using a street map, you can also locate where you are on the map to work out the best route to your destination. Or, if you're out in nature, you can look for features like a mountain or river that can help you determine where you are, and again, plan your route accordingly.

Another useful feature on most maps is the scale, which you will usually find in a corner somewhere. It looks a bit like a candy-striped barber pole, but its purpose is to show you how long a mile or kilometer is on the map. If you measure the distance between your current position and where you want to go, and compare it to the scale, you can calculate roughly how far you have to travel to get there.

With a map and a compass, you can work out how to get from nearly anywhere to nearly anywhere. You can even calculate how far apart your desired locations are and about how long it will take you to travel between the points!

Now that you know how compasses work, how they were invented, and how to use them with a map, it's easy to see why compasses are so essential and why they have been for so long. Without the compass, it would have taken a lot longer for explorers in history to find new and exciting places.

If Christopher Columbus hadn't followed his compass, trying to circumnavigate the world to reach India, he would never have landed in America. If we didn't have compasses, people like Robert Peary would never have reached the north pole. We wouldn't have shipping or air travel the way we do today. In fact, the world would be a lot more difficult to navigate altogether.

Fortunately, thanks to human curiosity and some very smart scientists throughout history, we do have magnets and compasses, and we can do all those things. So, let's move on and find out more about how compasses are made.

ONCE A YEAR, GO SOMEPLACE YOU'VE NEVER BEEN BEFORE.

– Dalai Lama

CHAPTER 2

COMPASS DESIGN & PARTS

You could make a compass the way the ancient Chinese did, by nailing a piece of iron to a board and floating it in a bucket. But that might not be too easy to carry and find your way around with!

Fortunately, we have much more modern compass designs these days, and you can buy some very fancy compasses.

In this chapter, we're going to look at the various parts and pieces that make up compasses. We will also consider some of the special types of compass that are out there. It's not strictly necessary to learn how a compass does what it does to use a compass properly – but it's always a good idea to know how the things we use work.

So, while you don't have to take things apart to discover their inner workings like a much younger me, you're about to learn how compasses are designed, made, and customized for specific jobs.

COMPASS DIRECTIONS

A compass always points to the north, and knowing where north is, is all you need to figure out where the other directions are.

Every compass is divided into the four major directions: **North**, **East**, **South**, and **West**.

Like any circle, the compass is also made up of 360 degrees. Each direction or quadrant is ninety degrees, or, as we call it in math, a "right angle."

Bet you never thought you would use geometry in the real world, but when it comes to directions (and many other things), that's very often exactly what you're doing!

REMEMBERING THE DIRECTIONS ON A COMPASS

The directions on a compass never change. North, east, south, and west are always in the exact same position relative to each other. So, if you know where they are on a compass, you don't even have to see the markings to know what each one is.

But how do you remember?

There are several mnemonics that help you to remember this. A mnemonic is a rhyme or story that helps you to remember important information. In this case, we will use some to help you remember the directions on a compass. For example, you can use any one of the following to recognize which order the directions are, going from north in a clockwise direction. The first letter of each word in the following sentences, stand for the first letter of a direction:

- **N**ever*(North)* **E**at*(East)* **S**oggy*(South)* **W**affles*(West)*
- **N**aughty **E**lephant **S**quirts **W**ater
- **N**ever **E**at **S**pider **W**ebs
- **N**ever **E**nter **Santa's** **W**orkshop
- **N**ever **E**nter **S**tinky **W**ashrooms

Choose whichever one you like or make one up of your own! Whatever makes it easy to remember the order of the directions is all you need!

COMMON COMPASS DESIGNS

As you can imagine, for a piece of equipment we've been working on for 2,500 years, there are many different kinds of compass out there! They all work in basically the same way, but some are a lot fancier than others. Here are 5 of the most common types of compasses around.

Standard or Basic Compass

A standard or basic compass is probably the one you have seen the most – or maybe even own!

A standard compass is remarkably simple. It has a casing, a backing marked with the directions, a pivot-mounted magnetic needle, and a plastic or glass cover that you can look through to use the compass.

These compasses don't have many bells and whistles like rotating bezels or fancy alignment tools. They're often very affordable and sometimes have a hook to allow you to attach them to a backpack when you're hiking or even to hang them off your house keys. Best of all, they offer a simple way to help you figure out where you are going!

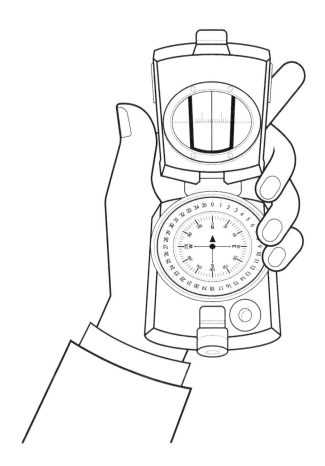

Sighting Compass

A sighting compass is a more sophisticated design that allows you to look at an object in the distance and see the compass reading at the same time. Most use mirrors to make this possible.

Sighting compasses are used by hunters, explorers, and the military to determine the direction to a particular target – whether that's a herd of antelope, an enemy base, or a specific mountain peak.

Some sighting compasses also include a special kind of tool known as a *clinometer*, which measures the angle of inclination, so you know the horizontal direction of the target and the vertical gradient that it is at.

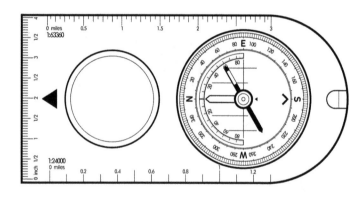

Baseplate Compasses

Baseplate compasses are what we will look at in more detail a little later.

These compasses are often liquid-filled and mounted on a baseplate (which is usually transparent to allow you to see a map below.) They are typically marked with directions and degrees, so you can take accurate bearings. In addition, they often include other features like ruler measurements or even tools that you can use when you're out exploring.

They're accurate, easy to use, and usually have a few extra features. This makes them great for hikers and explorers, who need to keep their backpack weight as low as possible!

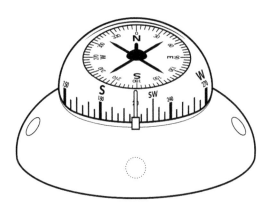

Marine Compasses

Marine compasses are a little different from the other types described here. What's unique about marine compasses is that their needle is fixed and stays stuck, but instead, the whole compass card floats on water. (*Like the old boards used by Chinese sailors!*)

Since the whole compass card floats, it allows for the compass to stay level while you're on choppy water. This way, you can still find north and navigate even while you bob unevenly up and down on the water.

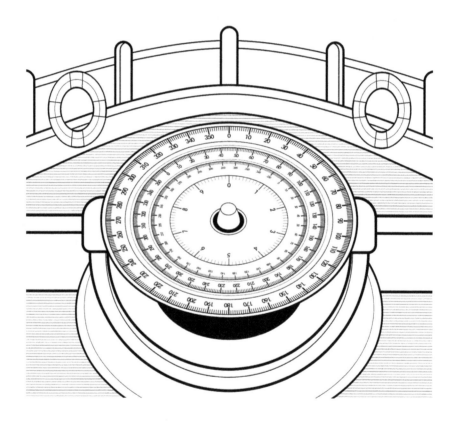

Gyrocompasses

Gyrocompasses are expensive and complicated electric compasses that are used on things like **really** big ships. Unlike magnetic compasses, they're not affected by magnetic fields, so they are very accurate. Aside from being expensive, they're also big and heavy, so they're not used for personal navigation.

ANATOMY OF A COMPASS

As you just learned, compasses come in a variety of sizes, shapes, and designs. Still, the basic parts of the magnetic compass are the same for all of them. These are:

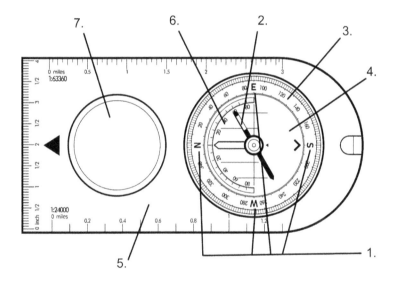

1. Cardinal Directions

All compasses are marked with the cardinal directions: North, East, South, and West.

Some will have secondary markings like NW, SW, SE, and NE, or degrees, but those aren't strictly necessary to tell where you're going.

2. Compass Needle

The compass needle is a magnet, and it is usually painted red and white.

Most compass needles are red for north and white for south.

3. Dial / Rotating Bezel

The dial or bezel of the compass is the part that has the degrees marked on it. Degrees are used to help us navigate more accurately.

4. Housing

The compass housing is the part of the compass that the needle is mounted in.

This usually includes things like red orienting lines, which help you align your compass on your map. There is usually also an orientation or direction of travel arrow. All of these parts help you make sure you're heading the right way.

5. Baseplate

The compass's baseplate is the flat part under the compass itself that you lay on your map. It may be opaque or transparent and often has additional markings like a ruler, which you can use to measure scale on your map.

6. Declination Scale

So we know that compasses point north, or to be more exact magnetic north. This is slightly different from true north, which you can see on maps. The declination scale helps you make the correction between these two slight differences.

The difference between magnetic north and true north is known as declination, and it differs depending on where you are in the world. The declination scale helps you to adjust your bearing from magnetic north to true north.

7. Magnifying Glass

A lot of maps have tiny details that might be hard to see. That's why many compasses have a magnifying glass built-in, so you can see smaller writing and measurements easily.

Sighting Mirror

If you are using a sighting compass, it will have a sighting mirror. This will allow you to look at an object that you want to navigate towards and still see your compass, so you can determine what direction the object is in.

SIMPLE PARTS, BIG IMPACT!

As you can see, there aren't any complicated parts on most compasses that people usually use. Yes, there are huge intimidating compass devices on ships and other oversized vehicles. Still, most of us will never use one of those.

This is part of the reason why compasses are so great. They're relatively uncomplicated and easy to make, which means everyone can learn to use one. They're also amazingly simple, with only one moving part, which means there's truly little that can go wrong with them. Although you still need to be a little bit careful, as we will discuss later.

But as simple as a compass is, in terms of design, they're hugely helpful and really have changed our world. This just shows that something doesn't have to be complicated, big, or expensive to make a great impact.

CREATIVITY IS LIKE A
COMPASS, EACH ONE HAS
ITS OWN, AND ALL POINT
TO THE NORTH.

– Efrat Cybulkiewicz

CHAPTER 3

NAVIGATION 101

Long ago, when people first started using compasses to navigate the world, huge parts of it were completely unknown and unexplored. In fact, some people still believed that the world was flat and that you could fall off the edge until fairly recently!

But we've come a long way since then, and there are very few parts of the world that we haven't mapped. At least on solid ground! There are still many parts of the ocean that are a mystery. Still, as technology like satellites and GPS become more sophisticated, we are even learning more about that.

That's good news for us, because it means that there are maps of nearly every part of the world. Modern maps are also very accurate because, unlike the old maps you see in pirate stories, they didn't have to be hand-drawn! Scales, directions, and features are marked precisely, making navigating today a lot easier than it used to be. Even if you leave sea monsters and falling off the earth out of the equation!

But, even with a map and knowing that the top of the map is always north, you still need a compass to make sure you know where north is. So welcome to navigation 101, where we'll get the very basics out of the way.

TYPES OF MAPS

No matter what, it's always a great idea to bring the right tool for the job. Maps are no different...

There are many different types of maps, and it's essential to use the right one to get to where you need to be. These are a few of the maps you might need to use to navigate around your world.

Physical Maps

Physical maps are maps of the world that show major geographical features, like mountain ranges and rivers. They're similar to the maps that early explorers used before there were cities and settlements, and when they used these kinds of features to orient themselves when they were traveling.

If you know the location of a particular mountain, for instance, and its position relative to the north pole, you can use it to keep yourself going in the right direction. Simply by making sure you keep it on the correct side of you when you're traveling.

Physical maps are usually very "zoomed out," though. So they might show the borders of countries, and maybe a few of the biggest city names, but they have very little other detail, and they're not great for modern-day navigation!

Topographical Maps

Topographical maps, as the name suggests, show the **topography** of an area. This means that they show what we call "contour lines," which are lines that show the height or elevation of a particular point.

These kinds of maps are often used when planning big construction projects, like roads, where mountains and valleys could get in the way of building.

While this can be useful to calculate the actual distance between two points (because a flat measurement isn't accurate if there are steep slopes involved), they're not usually used for the kind of navigation you will be doing.

Road Maps

Road maps are the kind of maps that we are most likely to use these days. They might come as one large sheet or, more often, as a printed "road atlas."

These maps allow us to see the major cities, towns, and points of interest of a particular area, or, on a more "zoomed in" scale, the streets and attractions in cities or neighborhoods.

If you are traveling around the world today, you will most likely be using a street map or a street atlas.

Other Maps

There are many other kinds of maps that show all kinds of information about the world. Time zone maps, for example, as the name suggests, show the various time zones in the world. Maps can also be used to graphically represent election results, political information, volcanic hazards, income distribution, and much more data.

If you're interested in the world, maps are a great way to learn more about how everything works graphically. So, if you've got some time, it's a great idea to spend some of it learning more about the different maps of your city, area or country, or the whole world!

HOW TO HOLD A COMPASS

Now that we covered a lot of the background information, we can start working on our compass. You might not know this, but how you hold a compass is especially important to get an accurate reading.

Compasses are designed to be used when they are level (which is why some compasses float on water!)

So, while there are different methods of holding a compass, the most important thing is to make sure that it is level when you use it.

One easy way to do this is to hold your hand out, level with the ground, and place the compass on your open palm. The orienting arrow should always be pointing away from you, in the direction you would travel if you were to walk straight ahead.

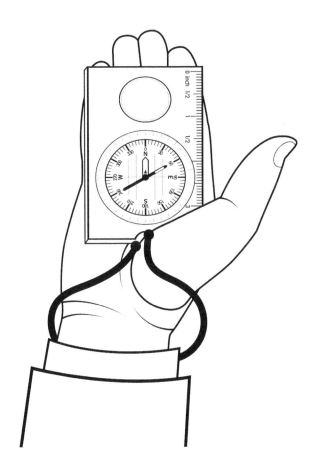

Once you're holding your compass correctly, you can slowly turn in place until the needle points towards magnetic north on the compass dial. Once that happens, all you need to do is adjust the declination to true north, and you're ready to start navigating!

BASIC STEPS FOR USING A COMPASS

Now that you know what the various parts of the compass are, how to hold it, and other general information, it's time to learn how to use it.

It's a good idea to get your practice using and reading a compass in your backyard or somewhere close to home. Just having a compass doesn't mean you can find your way home, so in this case, **DO** try this at home!

1. Make sure you have a compass and a map of where you want to go.

2. Place the map on a flat surface and your compass flat on top of it.

3. Remember that the top edge of the map is always north (unless it's otherwise indicated somewhere on the map with a compass rose.

4. Rotate the map and the compass until true north on your compass matches up with the compass rose, or your compass's true north point is pointing directly towards the top of your map.

5. If your desired location is marked on the map, you should be able to see which direction you need to go in. This is also known as your "heading."

6. Turn the dial of the compass until your heading lines up with the direction of travel arrow.

7. Now, place the compass flat on your palm and turn your body, holding it straight in front of you until the red north arrow points to the north marker on the compass dial.

8. If you now walk in the direction of the "direction of travel" arrow, you will be heading towards the direction you need to go.

If you can, it's a good idea to find a landmark in the distance that lines up with the direction you are headed in. This can be anything from a large building or sign to a big tree or mountain. Having a landmark like this will allow you to travel without needing to constantly look down at your compass.

You can check your compass as you go (and that is a good idea!), but if you have a large landmark to walk towards, you will be sure you're heading in roughly the right direction all the time, and you can just check and correct slightly as you go.

When you reach your chosen landmark, take out your map and compass, and do it all again.

WHERE TO USE A COMPASS

Even though your compass only has a few moving parts and is very reliable, there can still be some areas or situations where you need to double-check that everything works properly. There are certain locations where your compass might not work right. Here are some places or positions to avoid when you're using a compass:

- Close to any high-tension power lines. Since magnetism and electricity work closely together, the electrical current in the power lines can affect the accuracy of your compass.
- Near magnets or magnetic items.
- In places where there is a high iron content in surrounding rocks. This is not quite common, but

some places with rocks like iron ore, basalt, or meteorites can affect the way your compass works.

- Large vehicles. Cars, trucks, and RVs are made with steel bodies and parts, and steel is very magnetic. So if you use a compass right next to one of those, you could get an inaccurate reading.
- Fences or telephone wires. The metal used in the wires and the signal can make your compass less accurate.

If you notice that your compass needle doesn't seem to "settle" and it keeps moving around, you might be close to something that is interfering with your compass that you can't see. Try walking a short distance away, and check if it works better when you do.

ADVANCED NAVIGATORS AND COMPASS DIRECTIONS IN DEGREES

A compass needle can rotate freely in a circle and always looks to point towards magnetic north. Like any circle, the compass is made up of 360 degrees, and each direction or quadrant is ninety degrees, or, as we call it in math, a "right angle."

Your plate compass will have these degrees marked on the rotating bezel along with the cardinal directions. Because of this, you might have heard people referring to a direction in degrees as well. For example, someone might say that they need to head 40 degrees north-west. That would mean that they will go 40 degrees to the left of north, heading in a north-westerly direction.

Understanding the degrees on a compass helps you navigate to a location, but it is also very helpful for finding your way back. For example, let's say you successfully navigated your way to a landmark 45 degrees from your home. When you want to head back home, you only need to turn 180 degrees (half a circle). Then you know the compass will direct you back home. Look on your compass, and you can see the degrees on the opposite side of the 45 marking are 225. So your heading when walking back home would be 225 degrees.

Directions Based on the Mathematical Round Protractor

Sometimes, directions are also referred to based on the 360-degree mathematical compass. It is rare, but still great to know. So, in this case, north would be 90 degrees, west would be 180 degrees, south would be 270 degrees, and east would be both 0 and 360 degrees.

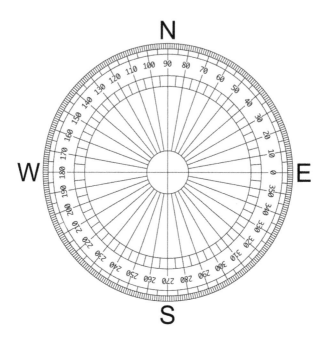

Each quadrant is 90 degrees, and by breaking the compass up this way, we can tell where a particular bearing would fall. For instance, because 150 degrees is between 90 and 180 degrees, we would know that that direction would fall between north and west or be in a north westerly direction.

That was a bit like a math class, right? A compass is a perfect example of how we use math and science in the real world!

TAKES A LITTLE PRACTICE

As you can see, the steps involved in using a compass are simple, it just takes a little practice to get the hang of the process.

Spend some time practicing with your compass, using these steps, to navigate to things in your neighborhood. Then go to a local park with your family, and test your navigation skills out there.

Using a compass is a lot like riding a bicycle. Once you know how to do it, you will never lose the skill!

Now that you know the basics of using a compass, though, it's time to take a closer look at some of the fun ways you can do just that.

THE WORLD IS A BOOK AND THOSE WHO DO NOT TRAVEL READ ONLY ONE PAGE.

- Saint Augustine

CHAPTER 4

LET'S GET OUT THERE!
GO OUT AND PRACTICE

Learning and reading about something new like a compass is definitely a lot of fun! Still, actually using your compass and exploring the world is even more fun — especially if you bring some friends along!

In this chapter, we look at some fun ways you can practice using your compass close to home before heading out into the wilderness with nothing but your compass and your wits. Some of these activities can be done by yourself, some with friends and some may require a parent or "referee".

While you are learning to use a compass, make sure someone always knows where you will be and where you are going. Stay close to home, and keep a charged cellphone and a GPS if you have one in your pocket or backpack. You don't have to use them unless you need to, but it's always better to be safe than sorry until you're completely confident in your abilities!

But now that we've got the safety tips out of the way, let's look at some of the adventures you can have.

PRACTICE MAKES PERFECT

You've probably heard the saying *"practice makes perfect"* at least a few times. It applies to everything – even using a compass!

So before you go out into the woods and trust your compass and map to get you home, you should spend some time getting really comfortable with using both of them.

Look around your neighborhood and find some local landmarks that really stand out, and then figure out what their heading is from your front yard. Is it out west? Could it be towards the south? Maybe it's something like north-east? If you know precisely where the familiar landmarks near your home are, you will always know how to make your way home.

You can mark these on a map or use them to draw your own map.

Treasure Hunt

Create a treasure hunt near your home, and use a map and compass to mark the location of the various items to be found.

Each location will have a package or "treasure" as well as the heading and distance for the next stage of the hunt. Instructions can be as simple as:

"Head 25 steps west from the back porch, then face north and take another 5 steps where you will find the next set of instructions."

You can ask a parent to set up a hunt for you, or if you are learning how to use your compass with one or more friends, you can each set up a numbered hunt and then draw a number out of a hat!

Whoever finds all of the objects or treasures on the list first wins, and you can decide what the prize will be!

Tour Guide!

Choose a location or landmark that you want your "tour" to get to.

Set a starting point for the tour, and then start setting up your directions. Figure out the heading of the landmark and then tell the person who is being guided which direction they need to go in and how far.

You could have one landmark or place a new heading and distance at each landmark so that the person who is doing the navigating knows where to go next.

With just a heading and distance, everyone should be able to figure out exactly where their next stop is!

Right Back Where you Started

Place an easy to identify object on the ground in a large field. This will mark your starting point.

Now use your compass to find magnetic north and walk 100 steps in that direction.

Turn your compass to 120 degrees, line up the direction of travel arrow and then walk 100 steps in that direction.

Turn your compass to 240 degrees, line up the direction of travel arrow again, and walk another 100 steps in that direction.

If your steps are about the same size, you should be just about exactly where you started. Did you get close, or were you a little off? How far off were you?

Compass Hide and Seek

Choose a few good hiding places in your area and draw a map, including each hiding place's coordinates.

Have one person from your group hide in each place on the map, and all the other kids are seekers. Take your compass with a notepad and pen, and race to find each hidden person and get a signature from them.

The first person to find all the hidden people and get a signature from each one wins the game.

Make a Beeline

This game is best played outside of the city, where you have some room to move! A local park or botanical garden will work well too.

Choose a start point for your beeline and an end point. Give everyone who is playing the bearing of their goal, and then place a prize of some kind in that location. It should be far enough away from the start that it can't be seen, and it's even more fun if there is some hiking involved!

Now give everyone a compass and the bearing of the prize, and let them head in that direction. Wherever possible and safe, players may need to climb over things like tree stumps or rocks.

Whoever gets to the prize first wins!

Learn Your Compass Points

This game doesn't require a compass and is all about practicing the location of cardinal and ordinal points.

You will need a basketball, a basketball court, and cones, or something else to mark the points of the compass.

Mark each of the cardinal points (North, East, South, and West) and the ordinal points (Northeast, Southeast, Southwest, and Northwest) on the court with a cone or marker.

Players form teams, and once they have, they take turns having the ball. One person calls out a direction, and the player with the ball must immediately go to the marker they think is correct. If they are correct, they may take a shot. If not, they must forfeit their shot.

Play until one team reaches a predetermined number of shots – and they are the winner!

Create a Navigation Course

This is a fun way for two people or teams to test their skills.

Each team should use a map and a compass to create their own navigation course.

Choose various landmarks and determine their bearing and distance. Then write down a list of instructions that your players need to follow to find the final destination. Place a small marker of some kind at each point on the trail so that players know they have found the right spot.

Now swap maps and get navigating!

Provide each player with the same map, a compass, and the list of instructions, and let them use the instructions to find their way to the finish line!

Orienteering – the Sport of Navigation

If you can find a formal orienteering organization in your city or town, you can sign up to try out the sport of orienteering.

Yes, there's a real sport that uses topographical maps and compasses! It's a race too, so it's pretty exciting.

Orienteers are all given the same map at the start of the race, and runners (or sometimes mountain bikers or canoeists) race to find their way around the course using the map, and of course, their compasses.

There's even an International Orienteering Federation and global championship events. So if you get really good at navigating with a compass and map, you can use your skills to win a major event!

THE MORE YOU PRACTICE, THE BETTER YOU GET

All of these ideas for practicing your compass navigation skills are a lot of fun, and a great way to spend some time with friends, get some fresh air and practice your navigation skills.

As with anything, the more you practice your navigation skills, the better they will get. Before you know it, you will be able to venture further out, onto hiking trails or into the wilderness, and use your compass and map to find your way around.

When you do, always make sure that someone knows where you are. Remember, just because you don't need a phone or

GPS to find your way around anymore, it's never a bad idea to have them along, just in case you need them.

BONUS ACTIVITY: USING YOUR WATCH AS A COMPASS

You might have heard that you can use your watch as a compass. This is true, and it's actually easier than you think!

You will need an "old-fashioned" wristwatch with the hours marked on the face and an hour, minute, and second hand to try this.

Method – (For the Northern Hemisphere):

1. Lay your watch flat horizontally.

2. Turn the watch until the hour hand aligns with the position of the sun.

3. The mid-way point between the hour hand (sun position) and the 12 o'clock marking is roughly where south is.

4. Directly opposite of that point is roughly where north is.

Method – (For the Southern Hemisphere):

1. Lay your watch flat horizontally.

2. Turn the watch until the 12 o'clock marker aligns with the position of the sun.

3. The mid-way point between the hour hand and the 12 o'clock marking (sun position) is roughly where south is.

4. Directly opposite of that point is roughly where north is.

This method is not as accurate as using a compass. This is because the sun's position will vary a little based on where you are and what season it is. Still, it is a good way to find out roughly where you are if you don't have a compass.

Make sure that the watch you are using is set correctly, though! This won't work if you use a watch that has stopped or is not set correctly!

When you have determined roughly where north and south are, use your compass to check how accurate your watch is at determining directions!

ANY DAY SPENT OUTSIDE IS A DAY WELL SPENT.

– *Anonymous*

CHAPTER 5

TIPS, TRICKS, AND FACTS

Now that you know how compasses are made, how they work, and how to use them to find your way around the world, it's time to look at some cool compass related tips, tricks, and facts.

Here are some things you might not know about the compass.

CARING FOR YOUR COMPASS

Magnetic compasses are pretty simple devices, with very few moving parts that you need to worry about. However, they still need to be cared for properly to make sure they keep working the way they are supposed to. Here are some important compass care tips to make sure yours stays in good shape!

1. Keep your compass far away from electronics and electrical devices. The magnetic field generated by things like computers and other devices can damage your compass by affecting the magnetism.

2. Store your compass away from hot places (like the car on a hot summer's day.) Heat causes expansion, and this can cause damage to the few moving parts that your compass does rely on.

3. Keep your cell phone and pocket radio far away from your compass. The speakers in these devices have magnets in them, and even though they are small, they can still demagnetize your compass enough to affect how it works.

4. Don't drop or bump your compass. Hard knocks can demagnetize the compass needle, making the compass less accurate or even, over time, stop it from working at all.

5. If you keep your compass in your backpack, don't store it close to metallic objects like pocket knives. The metal in these items can also affect your compass over time.

6. An excellent place to keep your compass to make sure it stays away from magnets, electricity, and metal items is on a lanyard around your neck or in a shirt pocket (with a button so it can't fall out!).

7. Try to keep your compass away from dust and sand. This can get under the rotating bezel and cause scratches and damage.

8. If your compass is liquid-filled, like many are, make sure there are no large bubbles in there. These can affect the working of the compass. If yours has a big bubble, it's time to replace it.

9. Check your compass from time to time. Choose a street that you know runs north to south, and stand on the curb facing north. Your compass should point straight up the road if everything is working correctly.

10. Finally, if the glass of your compass is scratched, you might be able to buy a special type of polish to take the cloudiness away. However, if it's cracked, it's almost impossible to fix, and it might be time for a new compass.

If your compass is not working properly, or you have noticed damage or wear on the markings, etcetera, it's usually better to replace it.

Some companies and specialists can fix compasses, but since a reasonably good one is quite affordable, having it repaired is probably more expensive.

You should always check that your compass is working properly before heading out on a trip where you know you will need to rely on it. A faulty compass can be a big problem when you are out hiking or exploring!

NAVIGATION TIPS

Knowing how to use a compass properly is a great tool, but there are some more useful tips that can make navigating with a compass and map a little easier. Here are some points to remember:

- Break your trip into smaller chunks. Instead of taking just one bearing to your final destination and hoping for the best (particularly over longer distances), break your trip into chunks, and choose smaller landmarks along the way. It's a lot easier to navigate accurately over shorter distances, and you can adjust as you go.
- When you do break your trip into chunks, take obstacles and natural features into account. The shortest distance isn't always the easiest route! Avoid very steep slopes or marshy areas wherever possible. You can always regroup and adjust your bearings when you reach a "checkpoint" along the way.
- Remember that the difference between magnetic north and true north differs by several degrees, which changes depending on where you are in the world. You should always find out what this angle is (known as declination) for the area you will be navigating in. So if you are traveling somewhere new and planning a hike, you might need to look this up again.

- Your compass will always point north. You need to move yourself and your maps to line up with that before figuring out which way to go.
- When you are on the move, check your bearing from time to time. Even if it seems like you're going in a straight line, you could actually be heading off course quite a lot. A quick check will let you adjust as necessary.
- If you aren't sure where you are when you're in the wilderness, try to get to higher ground, so you can spot a landmark that is marked on your map. This will help you figure out where you are and get the bearing of where you want to go.
- Remember that other things can help you to figure out where you are. Landmarks, rivers, and the sun's position can all help determine where you are. Then with a compass and a map, you should be able to find your way!

Even if you know how to use a compass, it's a very different thing to navigate in the wilderness than in your neighborhood. So if you are planning a hike somewhere, always make sure you go with someone who really knows their way around the trail. This can help you stay safe.

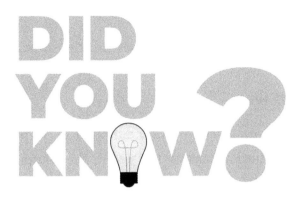

COMPASS TRIVIA

With such a long history, it's not really surprising that there are so many fascinating facts about compasses!

The Fortune Teller's Compass

You might think that the compass has always only been used for determining direction. But for many centuries after it was first developed, it was also used by fortune tellers and soothsayers when divining the future!

The Center of Your Compass Has a Name!

The center of your compass is called the "**compass rose**." It's also sometimes called a wind rose or "rose of the winds."

But They're Not All the Same!

You might think all compass roses are the same, but that's not true. The modern compass has 32 points on its compass rose, as does the old Arab compasses.

But eastern compasses can have either 24 or 48 points. So if you're in a different part of the world, the compass you use might look a little different. Luckily, they still work the same way!

Boxing the Compass

Want to test your knowledge of the compass the way old mariners did? Try "boxing the compass."

This requires you to name all the compass points, in order, starting at North and working clockwise. Can you do it? Try it, and race your friends to see who can do it correctly the fastest!

Compasses Can Be Calibrated for Use on Metal Ships

Remember when we said that you won't get an accurate reading from a compass if you're close to a lot of metal?

Well, modern ships are made of metal! This is why, when compasses are fitted in ships, they have to be calibrated or corrected. This is done by using special magnets and iron balls to correct the direction of the compass to point north as it should. They are fitted inside the casing of the compass.

The magnets used to adjust ship's compasses are called Flinders bars, and the metal balls are known as Kelvin spheres.

The Qibla Compass

Not all compasses are used to find the position of the north pole.

The Qibla compass is a special type of compass used by Muslims to find the position of Mecca. When Muslims pray, they face Mecca, so this helps them to find the right direction easily.

North By a Different Name?

A very long time ago, north wasn't marked by an N. Instead, it was marked by a spearhead and the letter T, which signified the Latin word *Tramantona*, which was the name for the north wind. This later became the fleur de lis, which you still see on many compasses and compass roses on maps today.

Magnetic North at the Equator

You know that magnetic north and true north are different, but did you know that they are much closer together when you use a compass at the equator? So the further north or south you go, the greater the difference will be.

Compass Points and Feng Shui

As we've mentioned, the Chinese were the first to figure out that magnetized metal could show them direction. Their compasses may have looked different (and pointed south rather than north), but they were identifiable as compasses.

It's no surprise then that Feng Shui, an ancient Chinese practice of geomancy that offers rules for aligning your surroundings with nature, includes many techniques related to the position of items and architecture. Many people still practice Feng Shui today. They move their furniture and décor items around their homes and other spaces to balance the flow of "chi" based on compass directions.

Fish Machine

The earliest mention of compasses in India referred to a "fish machine" or macchayantra. These were almost certainly Chinese in origin and were wet compasses consisting of a fish-shaped piece of magnetized metal on a floating board – which is where the name came from!

Astronomy

Compasses aren't only crucial for navigation and for early explorers. They were also used extensively by astronomers to chart the position of the stars. While the practice of astronomy itself isn't really a science, this did help us to identify constellations. Which was another way that early explorers and sailors used to determine where they were and where they needed to go.

Animal Compasses

Many types of fish, insects, and birds are believed to use the sun as an internal "compass" to help them maintain their direction when they are on the move.

Birds that migrate (and carrier pigeons!) are believed to use the earth's magnetic field to navigate. So that's how they always find their way home!

Magnetic Poles Move

You might think that the north and south poles are constant, but they aren't.

About 800,000 years ago, the poles were in opposite places. Since we first discovered the magnetic poles in the 19th century, they have moved nearly 622 miles or 1000 kilometers. They continue to move about 25 miles or 40 kilometers every year.

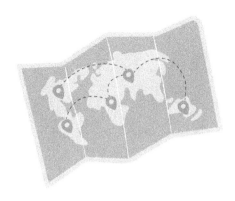

TRAVEL IS LIKE AN ENDLESS UNIVERSITY. YOU NEVER STOP LEARNING.

- Harvey Lloyd

CHAPTER 6

CREATE YOUR OWN COMPASS!

Now that you know what commercially available compasses are made of and what the various parts are, why not try to make your own compass? It's relatively easy to do, and you probably have all the stuff you need in your home.

YOU WILL NEED:

- *A sewing needle*

- *A red marker*

- *A magnet*

- *Wax paper*

- *Scissors*

- *A bowl of water*

Method:

1. Mark one end of the needle with the red marker. This will be the North point of your compass needle.

2. Rub the "north" side of your compass (which should also be colored red) along the marked side of your needle. You will need to do this about fifty times.

3. Turn the needle and magnet around and rub the "south" side of your compass on the south side of the compass needle.

4. Use a drawing compass or a large coin to draw a circle on the wax paper. The circle should be about 2.5cm or an inch in diameter.

5. Cut the circle out of the wax paper.

6. Thread the needle through the wax paper, pushing it through and then through again, as though you were sewing.

7. Float the circle on top of the water.

8. The magnetized "compass" needle will cause the circle to turn on the water's surface, and the red "north" point of the needle should point to magnetic north!

9. You can use your real compass to check how accurate your new homemade compass is!

This type of compass is exactly what the earliest Chinese sailors were using to figure out where they were going. Isn't it amazing that we can make something so useful out of things you have lying around your house right now?

LIVE YOUR LIFE BY A COMPASS, NOT A CLOCK.

- Stephen Covey

AFTERWORD

Now that we've reached the end of this compass guide, I hope that you've learned a lot about this relatively simple but endlessly fascinating piece of navigation equipment.

It's truly amazing that we've been using the compass in pretty much the same form for thousands of years and that we will continue doing it for many more.

With a compass in your pocket, as long as you know how to use it, you will never be truly lost, but remember that just knowing which way you're going isn't always enough. Always take a map with you if you're heading out to explore, so you have something to determine where you want to go. Then, the compass will show you how to get there!

Learning to use a compass can be a lot of fun, and it's a skill that you will have for life. Once you know how to read a compass, you will be able to navigate with one no matter where you are in the world. Of course, the position of true north may vary a little, and the maps will change, but the basics never do.

While you learn, take the time to try some of the other stuff in this book, like making your own compass or using your watch as a compass. If you can master skills like these, you will have even more navigation skills in your toolbox.

I hope you've enjoyed learning about how compasses work and that you're ready to start practicing with yours.

As always, however, remember that while compasses are great tools for finding your way around, there are always other safety precautions that you should take. For example, you should never go anywhere to test out your compass without telling someone where you are going. Even if you have all the compass skills you need, it never hurts to have a backup plan in the form of a cellphone, a GPS, or both.

Thank you for reading this guide, and happy trails!

MY NICKNAME FOR MY MOM WAS 'THE COMPASS.'

– Dane Cook

THANK YOU

Thank you for reading this book and allowing me to share my knowledge with you.

If you've enjoyed this book, please let me know by leaving an Amazon rating and a brief review! It only takes about 30 seconds, and it helps me compete against big publishing houses. It also helps other readers find my work!

Thank you for your time, and have an awesome day!

CPSIA information can be obtained
at www.ICGtesting.com
Printed in the USA
BVHW090809191222
654326BV00025B/317

9 783967 720785